Happy birth...

I hope you enjoy

ANIMAL
TALENTS

AND
OTHER POEMS

ANIMAL TALENTS

AND
OTHER POEMS

WRITTEN BY JOE GLOVER

ILLUSTRATED BY BEN BECKMANN

Published in 2021 by Joe Glover

A CIP catalogue record for this book is available from the British Library

ISBN 9798488526013

www.joeglover.co.uk

For my nephew, Rupert.

CONTENTS

Animal Talents   **11**

I'm Not a Dragon   **12**

Cats Can't Cook   **15**

Giraffe Warmers   **16**

Ginny   **17**

Spickley Span   **19**

Nathaniel the Spaniel   **20**

Writer   **21**

A Little Mouse   **23**

Rotten Luck   **24**

Challenge   **27**

Bee   **28**

Blackbird   **29**

The Bedroom   **31**

If Your Baby's Nearly Due   **35**

The School for All the Animals   **36**

Runner Bean   **39**

Bob McGoo   **40**

Octoclown   **43**

The Sailors   **45**

Fishy Fisherman   **47**

Claws   **48**

Certainty   **49**

Mr Tortoise   **51**

A Long Way to Walk   **52**

The Climb   **55**

ANIMAL TALENTS

Don't limbo with a snake
For it will always take first place,
And it's not worth racing cheetahs—
They're the best in any race.

Chameleons are rather good
At playing hide and seek,
So if you play against them
You'll be seeking them for weeks!

In a beauty contest
Nothing beats a butterfly.
A climb against a monkey?
You needn't even try.

An ostrich with an egg and spoon
Is faster than you'd think;
They'll beat you to the finish line
As quick as you can blink!

All animals have skills
That make them great at what they do,
And if you put your mind to it
You'll find that you do, too.

I'M NOT A DRAGON

Well hello little people,
You've a very lovely town,
But why are you all screaming?
Why such panic all around?

Who, me? I'm not a dragon!
Please don't run away in fear,
I'm just a friendly traveller,
No need for swords and spears!

Oh, gosh, you saw the fire
That was coming from my mouth?
I'm training for the circus
As I make my way down south.

The fire... it's just a trick!
A bit of theatre if you will.
Anyone could do it,
It just takes a little skill.

My claws? Now, don't be silly,
These are merely fingernails!
I really ought to trim them
For they scrape against my scales.

Scales? I'm such a scatterbrain!
My *skin* is what I meant.
Sometimes what my mouth says
Doesn't match with my intent!

And no, these aren't real wings,
These are just some fancy dress—
I'm heading to a party
And I want to look my best.

Oh dear, is that the time?
I think I'd better have some lunch,
And you look rather tasty,
Crunch! Crunch! Crunch!

CATS CAN'T COOK

Cats eat mice, but rarely with spice;
They normally have them quite bland.
You might find their food is not that nice,
When they cook, please offer a hand.

GIRAFFE WARMERS

To warm up a full-grown giraffe,
The best thing's a nice steamy bath.
It's a good thing they live where it's hot,
For a bath that large costs quite a lot.

GINNY

Though our dog is called Ginny
She has many names,
As having just one
Is a bore and a shame.

Call her Crinny or Crin-Cron
Or Ginner Von Crinner
(I honestly think
That last name's a winner!)

It might seem quite silly
But how could just one
Be enough for a dog
Who should not be outdone?

And if Ginny is Crinny,
And Crinny is Cron,
Then the names aren't that silly
Because they're all one.

SPICKLEY SPAN

Spickley Span was a very clean man,
Yes, a very clean man indeed.
If he ever found muck,
He would shout out, "Yuck!"
And clean with incredible speed.

Spickley saw that beneath his floor
Was hiding lots of mud,
So he pulled up the wood
Right beneath where he stood
And he scrubbed and he scrubbed and he scrubbed.

He cleaned out a hole like a burrowing mole
Going deeper than even a miner,
He went so far down
That the world flipped around,
For he'd cleaned all the way through to China!

NATHANIEL THE SPANIEL

Nathaniel the spaniel
Was all in a tangle
Because he was chasing his tail.
He twisted and coiled to get a good angle:
He simply could not bear to fail.

But once it was caught
And he had what he sought,
Off he was ready to trot,
Though it didn't turn out quite as well as he thought
As he found he was tied in a knot!

WRITER

There once was a very smart writer
Who spoke to the desk lamp beside her.
She taught it to read
(Impressive indeed!)
And then found that she'd made the lamp brighter!

A LITTLE MOUSE

A tiny little mouse
Was living in a bottle bank.
He didn't mind at all
That it really rather stank.

He played a brass trombone
In his home next to the street,
And he loved to snack on liquorice,
In fact, it's all he'd eat.

Some say a panda was his friend
But don't believe a word.
A mouse befriending pandas?
Why that's just plain absurd!

ROTTEN LUCK

Poor Anna's luck was rotten,
Things hadn't gone her way.
She'd lost her shoe
Then trod in poo…
Really not her day!

"When did my luck go bad?" she asked,
And stopped awhile to think.
She took it out,
And gave a shout
On account of its powerful stink.

"It's gone mouldy!" she cried to herself,
"My luck has turned stinky and sour!
The smell is so strong,
Just a whiff of the pong
Could easily wilt any flower!"

But later, when she was at home—
Inspiration struck!
With a board and a knife
She cut off a slice
Of the terribly pungent luck.

She popped it in her mouth,
(For she'd always done as she pleased)
And cried out "What taste!
Not a crumb shall I waste,
For it's even better than cheese!"

CHALLENGE

Try to read straight through this list;
Your brain will burn, your tongue will twist.
Watch your parents, uncles, aunts,
Have a go, and find they can't!

Write and weight, wrong and white,
Right and rate, throng and fight.
Fury, furry, bury, berry,
Brainy, zany, many, any.
Worry, sorry, jolly, lorry,
Hurry, holly, holy, brolly.
Foal and foul and meal and maul,
Shell, shawl, sell, and shall and stall.
You and owe and own and ewe,
Law, lie, lilo, lay, low, loo.
Touch, tough, trough, and trout, thou, though,
Through and thought and slow, sue, sew.

Made it through without a stumble?
Most will end up in a jumble!
Bonus points if you can read
This list correctly when at speed!

BEE

The humble bumble,
Busy bee,
Makes his honey busily.
Being busy tastes so sweet
Because he's earned the food he'll eat.

BLACKBIRD

Blackbird soars on morning light
As daybreak lifts her early flight.
She sings her song
To say, "So long,
And farewell!" to the night.

THE BEDROOM

Cat prowled around the bedroom,
Parading her domain.
Though Dog would like to enter
Cat ensured that he refrained.

Dog whined out in the hallway,
"Let me sleep upon the bed?
I'll make no noise or nuisance
Just curl up and rest my head!"

"Dear Dog," said Cat, "I understand
That you may feel frustration,
But as you know, your company
Is far beneath my station.

It simply wouldn't do
To let you come into the room;
Just think of all the scandal
And of what folk may presume."

"Oh, please!" begged Dog with widened eyes,
"You'll not know that I'm there."
A questing paw crept forward
Despite Cat's fiercest glare.

Atop the bed, with hair on end,
Cat cried, "Have you gone mad?
You must go no further!
This is really very bad!"

Said Dog to Cat, "It's not my fault,
I simply can't resist:
I hear the bedsheets calling,
I'm afraid I must insist."

Cat looked down in horror
As Dog stalked through the door.
He knew he shouldn't be there
Yet he crossed the bedroom floor.

"I warn you, Dog, not one more step,
You know this ends in tears.
If you dare climb upon this bed
I'll more than box your ears!"

"I'm sorry Cat, but here I come,
It's something I can't help."
Up he jumped and with a swipe
Cat made the poor mutt yelp.

Said Cat, "It isn't easy,
But I mustn't be ignored.
I think it's best you leave now
So that order is restored."

"Quite right." said Dog, "I understand.
I don't know what I thought.
I'll come back here tomorrow
And I'll prove the lesson taught!"

Cat despaired: "Oh, foolish Dog,
You do this every day!
Why is it that you never learn
That out there you must stay?"

IF YOUR BABY'S NEARLY DUE

Mum ate an extra helping
Of Dad's legendary stew.
She said that it was needed
For the baby as it grew.

But Mum, she got quite greedy,
Her appetite too bold,
So the baby grew too quickly
And it came out tall and old!

"Hello Mum" said Baby,
"I'll be off to work today;
The mortgage doesn't pay itself,
We've lots of bills to pay."

And so a word of warning
If your baby's nearly due:
If you eat too much, it's certain
That you'll find they over-grew!

THE SCHOOL FOR ALL THE ANIMALS

Have you ever wondered
How birds all learn to fly?
Or how snakes know to shed their skin
When it gets tight and dry?

How do monkeys learn to climb?
Who trains the stubborn mule?
You might not know the answer:
There's a secret hidden school.

The pupils all are creatures
With bright feathers, scales, or fur,
An orangutan is teacher
Who they all address as 'Sir'.

With each new year arrives a group
Of animals to teach.
The great ape will address them all
With his well-practised speech:

"Welcome class, please take your seats
And give me your attention.
I'll start by stating all our rules
So you'll avoid detention!

No horseplay in the hallways,
And cats mustn't caterwaul.
From birds I'll have no silly larks—
I mean it, none at all!

And please, no monkey business,
Copy cats, or badgering.
Pigheadedness I'll punish
Else you'll not learn anything!"

When the speech is finished
Comes the time for their first lesson.
The academic year begins
For school is then in session.

The animals will learn about
The fields and skies and trees.
The older ones are even taught
About the birds and bees!

So if you ever think your pets
Have things they need to know,
The school for all the animals
Is the only place to go!

RUNNER BEAN

Look at this veggie,
The swiftest of beans,
A number one runner,
All tall, lean, and green.

Sorry, poor veg,
You're still slower than me;
I'm going to catch you
And eat you for tea!

BOB MCGOO

Poor old Mr Bob McGoo!
He left to go to Waterloo,
But lost his map
And so the chap
Wound up at London Zoo.

Bob McGoo! Bob McGoo!
What's a man like Bob to do?

Poor old Mr Bob McGoo!
Pesky monkeys at the zoo
Had pinched his keys
Like common thieves
And nabbed his wallet, too!

Bob McGoo! Bob McGoo!
What's a man like Bob to do?

Poor old Mr Bob McGoo!
He held his breath and turned all blue.
The doctor said
To stay in bed
Till twenty thirty-two!

Bob McGoo! Bob McGoo!
What's a man like Bob to do?

Poor old Mr Bob McGoo!
His doctor's bills were overdue,
So in a huff
He packed his stuff
And moved to Timbuktu!

OCTOCLOWN

Come one, come all, the time is near!
It comes but only once a year,
Prepare to laugh and clap and cheer:
The circus is in town!

We've wondrous sights for eager eyes,
Guaranteed to mesmerise!
To miss this chance would be unwise,
It's time to come on down!

We've tightropes, tricks and magic acts,
Strongmen, stilts, and acrobats,
Musicians, mimes, and even snacks!
You see, we've got it all!

See tumbling, twirling, spinning, diving,
Aerial stunts with perfect timing,
Eating fire and yet surviving,
Human cannonball!

But in our show, the best by far:
An octopus—our juggling star!
His skills have truly set the bar;
He'll flip around your frown!

Eight limbs combined with style and flair
Make him a clown beyond compare,
You won't find better anywhere—
Huzzah for Octoclown!

He whips his tentacles to throw
All sorts of objects to and fro,
They whirl up like a tornado
But still there's more to see:

He throws the mimes up in the air
Then strongmen next to join them there,
He juggles all with skill and care,
Defying gravity.

A penny for the entrance fee:
A bargain, surely you agree!
Now go enjoy our show with glee:
The greatest show around!

It's starting now, you're almost late!
Just step right in, don't hesitate!
Please take a seat and see the greatest
Feats of Octoclown!

THE SAILORS

Seven singing seamen sailed
Aboard a battered boat,
Until one day the boat's hull failed
And simply ceased to float.

They sank beneath the surface
Past the Point of Porlock Bay;
The sailors' new-found purpose
Was to hold their breath all day.

Underwater and a wreck,
Their ship would never sail;
Instead they stood on deck,
Then were swallowed by a whale.

But the sailors didn't die
When eaten as a feast,
And now the men all dwell
In the belly of the beast.

FISHY FISHERMAN

A fisherman was fishing
For some fish while out at sea,
And the fish that he was fishing for
Were fishy as can be.
So fishy were the fish
That when he hauled those fish aboard
The fishy fish were salted
And to stop the smell, were stored.
The fisherman, he fought to fight
The very fishy smell
Because aboard a fishing boat
The fish smell's hard to quell.
But alas, our fishing fisherman
Will always smell of fish,
Although to smell of something else
Is his only wish.

CLAWS

See the cat,
Stroke his fur,
Watch him stretch,
Hear him purr.
Touch his ears,
Tail or paws
For too long:
Risk the claws!

CERTAINTY

One thing I'll say with certainty:
You're older than you used to be.
You first turned one, then two, then three
(Your age goes up and up, you see).

MR TORTOISE

"Come now, Mr Tortoise,
You're making me quite late.
If you could hurry up a bit
That really would be great."

Mr Tortoise turned and said,
"A minute more, I pray.
It's hard to put my jacket on—
My shell gets in the way!"

A LONG WAY TO WALK

It's come to my attention
That you're moving far away;
To get to you on foot
I'll have to walk all night and day!

And so to see you two times
Is two days and then two nights,
But then my journeys back
Mean that I'll have to walk that twice!

So four days and four nights
Of tireless walking to and fro
Makes two times I can see you,
Which is surely worth a go.

Though is that quite enough?
I think I'd like to see you more.
Two visits seems too few,
I'd rather three or maybe four.

If walking for eight days and nights
Four times will I arrive,
We may as well add on one more
And round it up to five.

So ten days and ten nights to walk,
That really sounds a pain!
To save some time I think it's clear
That here you should remain.

THE CLIMB

Once upon a long lost time
There lived a boy who loved to climb.
Never happy on the ground
The young boy thus was often found
Out scaling walls or in the trees,
For these things he could climb with ease.

One day, when walking in the woods
He saw atop a hill was stood
A tree so great and broad and tall
It made all other trees look small.
So great, in fact, was this tree's height
The top was far beyond his sight.

The boy knew without any doubt
His destiny was calling out,
So then and there he made a vow
That he would find a way somehow
To climb and climb and never stop
Till he had reached the very top.

High he climbed, and higher still,
Using all his strength and skill,
Until, at last, he'd climbed so high
His outstretched hand could brush the sky.
The final branch was reached at last
Yet he continued right on past.

He chose to be both brave and bold
And used a cloud as his foothold.
It held his weight—he climbed aloft,
Then onwards through the clouds so soft
And out into a great vast space
Where hung the moon in all its grace.

The next step was his bravest yet
And one he'll surely not forget,
For he leaped high with all his might
Towards Earth's rocky satellite...
And landed there—his climb was done!
The challenge met and he had won.

Now there he lives above all things
And of the climb he fondly sings,
So, if you listen well at night,
And when the moon is shining bright,
You might just hear his distant songs
Of how he found where he belongs.

THANKS FOR READING!

FIND OUT MORE AT
JOEGLOVER.CO.UK

Printed in Great Britain
by Amazon